AF270668

Barbie in the 1970s

DiscoverRoo
An Imprint of Pop!
popbooksonline.com

by Elizabeth Andrews

popbooksonline.com/seventies

abdobooks.com

Published by Pop!, a division of ABDO, PO Box 398166, Minneapolis, Minnesota 55439. Copyright © 2025 by Abdo Consulting Group, Inc. International copyrights reserved in all countries. No part of this book may be reproduced in any form without written permission from the publisher. DiscoverRoo™ is a trademark and logo of Pop!.

Printed in the United States of America, North Mankato, Minnesota.

052024
082024

THIS BOOK CONTAINS RECYCLED MATERIALS

Cover Photo: The Strong National Museum of Play

Interior Photos: Getty Images, Shutterstock Images, Design Bay Productions, Associated Press, Alamy Stock Photo, The Strong National Museum of Play, Terrence Antonio James/TNS/Newscom, Oliosi/Polaris/Newscom, Splash News/Mattel/Newscom

Editor: Grace Hansen

Series Designer: Victoria Bates

Library of Congress Control Number: 2023947574

Publisher's Cataloging-in-Publication Data

Names: Andrews, Elizabeth, author.

Title: Barbie in the 1970s / by Elizabeth Andrews

Description: Minneapolis, Minnesota : Pop!, 2025 | Series: Barbie through the decades | Includes online resources and index

Identifiers: ISBN 9781098246266 (lib. bdg.) | ISBN 9781098246822 (ebook)

Subjects: LCSH: Barbie dolls--Juvenile literature. | Toys--History--Juvenile literature. | Nineteen seventies--Juvenile literature. | Toys--Social aspects--Juvenile literature. | Popular Culture--Juvenile literature.

Classification: DDC 688.722--dc23

*Scanning QR codes requires a web-enabled smart device with a QR code reader app and a camera.

TABLE OF

Contents

Chapter 1
Barbie's Beginnings

Humans have made dolls for thousands of years. At first, dolls were made of clay, straw, or other natural materials. As the world changed, so did dolls. The toys got more detailed and exciting. In 1959, the fashion doll, Barbie, hit store shelves. The doll game was never the same.

Barbie's original
striped swimsuit
was inspired by
fashions worn in
the 1950s.

Ruth Handler was the creator of Barbie. Ruth and her husband owned the toy company Mattel Creations. Ruth noticed that children's dolls were mostly baby dolls. She believed growing girls didn't want to play with babies. They wanted dolls that encouraged them to dream of their futures.

Ruth Handler was born in Denver, Colorado, in 1916.

Mattel released the first Barbie in 1959. She wore a black-and-white swimsuit, black high heels, white sunglasses, and gold earrings. Barbie was a teenage fashion model from Willows, Wisconsin. She cost $3. Her extra outfits ranged between $1 and $5.

The Handler family

Barbie was a hit! In the first year, Mattel sold 350,000 dolls. Soon customers were asking for more. Mattel went on to create friends, dreamhouses, cars, and more than 250 careers for Barbie. Ruth was right. Children did like grown-up dolls. Their imaginations grew with Barbie!

The first Barbie appeared passive and gentle. She fit into the late 1950s female tradition of **homemaking** and beauty **trends**. Some of the first Barbies included Barbie Learns to Cook and Suburban Shopper Barbie. However, Ruth wouldn't keep Barbie in the home for long.

Suburban Shopper Barbie, 1959

Living in the Real World

In the 1970s, the United States was becoming more **diverse**. More people were moving to larger cities. **Baby boomers** were entering the workforce in great numbers. This included around 43% of women 16 years of age and older. More women were working than ever before!

DID YOU KNOW?

The US passed Civil Rights laws in the 1960s. The laws helped Black Americans join the workforce.

One of the purposes of the Civil Rights Act of 1964 was to end the unfair treatment of people based on race, gender, and religion.

Women earned less money than men doing the same job.

Many women were turning away from the traditional role of **homemaking**. They explored jobs in business, medicine, sports, and the arts. Some even became government leaders. As more women went to work, it became clear that they weren't treated the same as men. The Women's Rights Movement demanded equal opportunities and pay.

Americans also noticed that the Earth was being treated poorly. The first-ever Earth Day was held on April 22, 1970. Students and scientists joined together to spread the word about conservation. The Clean Air Act was updated twice in the 1970s to fight air pollution. Young people were changing the world for the better!

Conservation is the care and protection of the natural world for the future.

Popular entertainment was changing in the 1970s too. Music was getting louder and rock bands, such as The Rolling Stones and Fleetwood Mac, took over radio waves. **Disco** was also popular!

Professional sports gained more fans as **ESPN** came to television screens. The 1976 Summer Olympics was held in Canada. US sports fans felt they were a part of the action.

Rumours *by Fleetwood Mac, 1997*

Olympic swimmers Wendy Boglioli, Jill Sterkel, Kim Peyton, and Shirley Babashoff won gold medals for the USA.

Seventies Barbie Fashion

Barbie dolls that hit shelves in the early 1970s often had some kind of **gimmick**. Some dolls talked when a string on their body was pulled. Some came with hairpieces to trade in and out. Quick Curl Barbie and friends had wire in their hair to help style it in all kinds of ways!

Busy Barbie had hands that could grasp various things. She came with a bag, record player, phone, and cups.

In 1971, Mattel released a group of dolls led by Malibu Barbie. Malibu Barbie was different from Barbies before her. She had long, honey-blonde hair, tan skin, an

Malibu Barbie's friends included PJ, Christie, and Ken.

open smile, and eyes that looked straight ahead for the first time ever. She also wore less makeup. Malibu Barbie and her friends have become a favorite group of dolls for collectors.

Barbie's Friend Ship was released in 1972. It folded into a carrying case.

Flying High

Airplane travel became more common in the 1970s. Planes got bigger and could hold more people. Ticket prices were cheaper than ever before. First-class tickets were the most expensive. People were treated to food, drink, and a comforable lounge area. By 1972, half of Americans had traveled by plane.

Live Action Barbie could move her neck, arms, waist, and legs!

Live Action Barbie on Stage was also released in 1971. She was dressed in **iconic** hippie fashion. Many young people of the decade were wearing looser clothes and groovy patterns. Dressing Barbie in the **trends** of the time helped young girls imagine themselves as grown-ups just as Ruth wanted.

Live Action Barbie and Ken, 1971

In 1977, Superstar Barbie was released. She had a new face, blue eyeshadow, and a wide smile. This Barbie was designed to look like television stars of the time. She had earrings, a necklace, and a pink boa. Superstar Barbie matched the **disco** trends of the late '70s. More glamorous styles were in!

Superstar Barbie and Ken, 1977

CHAPTER 4

Barbie Gets Real

Barbie's fashions mirrored the changing **trends** in the real world. Clothes were cheaper in the 1970s. This made it easier for people to express themselves through their clothing.

Famous musicians made round glasses trendy.

23

Young people wore a lot of denim. They also wore tie-dye, patchwork, and **crocheted** pieces. Most fashions were inspired by famous musicians, such as Joni Mitchell, Elton John, and Cher.

Children related to people in the real world through their Barbies. Ruth Handler wanted to make sure the dolls they played with were just as exciting as famous stars of the time.

Deluxe Quick Curl Barbie and The Now Look Ken, 1976

Donny and Marie Osmond

Siblings and musicians Donny and Marie Osmond were the youngest people to host a variety show. Donny and Marie would ice skate, sing, and perform funny skits. Their show aired every Friday beginning in 1976. Mattel released the Donny and Marie dolls the same year.

Gold Medal Barbie, 1975

Throughout the 1970s, women made a name for themselves in sports. Gold Medal Barbie was released in 1975. She wore a red, white, and blue swimsuit and came with a gold medal. Gold Medal Barbie got kids excited about American athletes just as the Summer Olympics were taking place.

In 1972, a law called Title IX was passed. It said a person could not be prevented from playing a sport based on their gender.

The Women's Rights Movement encouraged girls to take jobs dominated by men. Before 1970, only six percent of people in US medical schools were women. By the mid-'70s, that number rose to 16 percent! Surgeon Barbie was released in 1973. She wore scrubs, a stethoscope, and a mask. She also came with a lab coat, diploma, and printed X-ray.

Barbie Country Camper, 1971

Like much of the world, Barbie also wanted to save the planet! Mattel released the Barbie Country Camper for Barbie and her friends. Children could imagine getting outside and enjoying all that the natural world had to offer. It helped inspire young children to care for nature and the planet.

Barbie and friends became even more popular during the 1970s. Mattel was finding new and creative ways to inspire children. The next decade would be even bigger and better!

Barbie Country Camper's box said, "A home for Barbie wherever she explores the great outdoors."

Making Connections

TEXT-TO-SELF

Have you ever played with Barbie or her friends?

If so, what kind of life did you imagine for them?

If not, what kind of life would you imagine?

TEXT-TO-TEXT

Have you read any books about other toys?

What did those toys have in common with

Barbie? How were they different?

TEXT-TO-WORLD

The first Earth Day was held in 1970. It is a

holiday that encourages people to care for the

environment. With an adult, research a way you

can help care for the environment. Write a few

sentences about what you discovered.

Glossary

baby boomers — a generation of people born from about 1946 to 1964.

crocheted — made with a crochet hook. Crochet is needlework made with a hooked needle that pulls the thread or yarn in a pattern of connected loops.

disco — a type of dance music or a night club where people dance to disco music.

diverse — made up of people or things that are different from each other.

ESPN — short for Entertainment and Sports Programming Network. A TV network that shows sports.

gimmick — a trick or device intended to attract attention.

homemaking — the job of caring for a household by cooking, cleaning, and raising children.

iconic — widely known or recognized easily.

trend — a current style or preference especially concerning clothing.

Index

popbooksonline.com/seventies

*Scanning QR codes requires a web-enabled smart device with a QR code reader app and a camera.